D1074713

DAVID HANKS

DOWN BY THE FEED MILL

The Past and Present of America's Feed Mills

and

Grain Elevators

Schiffer Publishing Ltd

4880 Lower Valley Road • Atglen, PA 19310

Published by Schiffer Publishing, Ltd.
4880 Lower Valley Road
Atglen, PA 19310
Phone: (610) 593-1777; Fax: (610) 593-2002
E-mail: Info@schifferbooks.com
Web: www.schifferbooks.com

For our complete selection of fine books on this and related subjects, please visit our website at www.schifferbooks.com. You may also write for a free catalog.

Schiffer Publishing's titles are available at special discounts for bulk purchases for sales promotions or premiums. Special editions, including personalized covers, corporate imprints, and excerpts, can be created in large quantities for special needs. For more information, contact the publisher.

We are always looking for people to write books on new and related subjects. If you have an idea for a book, please contact us at proposals@schifferbooks.com.

CONTENTS

PREFACE

A summer evening in Grant, Michigan. The railroad station and the water tank face the railroad track, with the feed mill across the way—a common arrangement in many small towns. This is a quiet time of day, but the evening train heading for the resorts to the north will be coming through soon and there will be citizens sitting on the bench by the crossing to watch it pass.

One day in Imlay City, I spoke with Gene Gibbard, operator of the Gibbard Brothers mill. "If you want to find the feed mill in any town, just go down to the railroad and look up and down the track for the tallest thing you can see," he said. "That'll be the mill." And that's how I found many of the mills whose portraits grace these pages.

This book is intended as a review, in words and images, of select feed mills in the southern half of Michigan's Lower Peninsula. These mills, past and present, may number in the hundreds, and they are remarkably similar to those found throughout the United States. Dating to the early 1800s, they vary in size and configuration; no two are exactly alike. Their design was based on local conditions depending on the type and volume of crops grown in the area. The owner of a planned mill was probably his own contractor and set the requirements for the size and layout based on his experience and local business protocols. He typically led a group of carpenters to his building site, used a stick to scratch a rectangle in the dirt, and said, "Well, boys, we're going to build ourselves a mill here, about this size." Later, in the early 1900s, there were engineering firms that specialized in feed mill design and construction.

The region's first settlers were from New England and brought some of their place names with them, which is why we find names like Vermontville, Vergennes, Portland, Woodbury, and Chelsea. The later Europeans gave us Westphalia from the Germans, Zeeland from the Dutch, and the Irish name Parnell. The New England contingent was responsible for the layout of the towns. The domestic architecture and the frequent inclusion of a village green are examples of this heritage.

Years of poking about resulted in the collection of images here. Several of the structures have disappeared, the inevitable result of constant change. Others have been enlarged. You won't find a comprehensive history accompanying each photograph, as most of them would read very much the same, with clouded histories, frequent changes of ownership, and sadly, bankruptcies.

A feed mill may be just a routine entity in a town, but everyone there will know something about it and be willing to comment on it. One poignant observation came from a boy of about ten who took an interest in my struggles with a camera. "What are the pictures for?" he asked. When I explained my mission and asked if he lived nearby, he indicated a house just up the street. I commented that it must be interesting to watch the comings and goings at the mill. This prompted him to reply with what may have been an echo of his elders' opinions. "Well" he said, "you don't get much peace and quiet if you live down by the feed mill."

INTRODUCTION

HOW IT ALL BEGAN: THE WHITE DOORKNOB

One summer morning in 1989 I stopped for gas in the town of Chelsea. Across the road from the gas station was a small, old railroad station, whose quaintness prompted me to photograph it. When I was finished photographing, an ancient, weatherbeaten building caught my eye across the railroad track. It was uninteresting except for a white porcelain doorknob on the dark, unpainted and sunless side of the decrepit building. The doorknob was gleaming like a beacon. Crossing the weedy track, I became more fully aware of the building's decayed state and the presence of two artifacts nailed to it: a rusted sign that read "Calf Manna" and an equally rusted thermometer that advertised Mail Pouch chewing tobacco.

Comstock Park

The Calf Manna sign was vaguely familiar and suggested the building dealt in farm supplies. The deep textures of the old place, its apparent neglect, and that insistent white doorknob—the only thing that didn't reflect the building's age—caused me to linger after I captured it with the camera. I also noticed a rake and shovel hanging on the back wall. There was no time for further study and so it was back in the car and on the road.

Weeks later I developed the film and found that the photo of the doorknob was the most intriguing picture on the roll. I made a print and, viewing it in the light, was both surprised and delighted, but I wasn't yet moved to go on a search for more doorknobs.

Some time later I happened to pass by a feed mill, or the remains of one, near my home. I wondered if it, too, had any photographic opportunities to offer. This mill happened to be in Comstock Park, a contiguous suburb of Grand Rapids, and it had been surrounded with residential and commercial building with the consequent loss of farmland. The mill had tried to hang on by selling garden supplies and pet food, but the land had become too valuable to resist its being sold to developers. When I revisited it with a camera, it had closed. I was enchanted and took time to explore and evaluate the subject.

The property was overgrown with weeds, but it seemed more interesting that way. It must have been then and there that I decided there was something to this feed mill thing. I knew there was an abandoned mill in Grand Rapids on Walker Avenue because it was in the neighborhood where I had grown up. It too had been swallowed by urban development.

Van Ess & Schreuder Feed Mill and Building Supplies, Grand Rapids

As old as the Walker Avenue mill was, the area must have been farmland at one time. A story in the local newspaper was headlined, "Last Mill in Area to Close." I'd ridden my bicycle past it many times on the way to a baseball field. The only note I made of it then was the perilous way it leaned over the sidewalk. Now older but certainly no wiser about feed mills, I returned to the old neighborhood with a camera for a more studied look. The building's wedge shape was a response to the triangular property. The photographs I made were the start of what would become a large collection.

From old insurance records I learned the old mill had been operated as Van Ess and Schreuder in 1904, but there was no record of its earlier history. So, I embarked on a slow and unmethodical search for more mills. After learning where mills were typically located, I not only found more mills, I was amazed at how many there were.

They were mostly in small towns and villages, eight to ten miles apart. This seems logical given the pre-automobile era in which they were established. A farmer would not want to drive his team of horses pulling a fully loaded wagon more than five miles to a mill, especially on a hot day, and then drag a wagon loaded with supplies back to the farm, a ten-mile round trip. Mill hands would have walked to work, and so they lived in the town.

The trick to locating feed mills soon became apparent. Large incoming and outgoing loads could only be handled by railroad. If you follow the route of a railroad, operational or abandoned, you are likely to find a mill or its remains. When trucks became a practical alternative to train cars after, say, 1920, feed mills sprang up farther from the railroads.

As my photography collection of mills grew, so did my knowledge of the subject. It became apparent that the feed mill business was much more complex than the building exteriors suggest. The Grand Rapids Library and local historical societies have a remarkably large archive of photographs made by dedicated and skillful amateur photographers. In perusing them I was fascinated that feed mills of 100 years ago, and more, were still to be found today, often not much changed from their original appearance.

What is the attraction of documenting old feed mills? Maybe it's a sense of saving something we know will cease to exist. This is what we experience when we look at the photo of the Union Elevator and Feed Mill. Collections of old photographs show up from time to time and are welcomed as important documents from an often fascinating past.

Photographing feed mills has taken me outdoors in fine weather and foul, in heat and cold. I have been a tourist in small towns and villages that I would otherwise never have visited and have seen interesting things that others pass by without a glance. I ask that each photograph be accepted as a reflection on the object itself. Each mill was studied closely to portray it in its most interesting aspect, and I chose to ignore or include certain elements. My hope is that the reader will experience a sense of being transported to times and places that we may not see again. After all, we are travelers both through space and time.

This photo of Union Elevators and Feed Mills was made in 1890 and is from the archives of the Grand Rapids Public Library. It was located in downtown Grand Rapids, which had a population of 75,000 at the time. The fact that the feed mill occupies valuable land in the business district attests to its value to the community.

Three Mills in Time

GONE . . . EDMORE MILL

Edmore, Michigan, is known as a production center for grain, corn, potatoes, and beans. At one time it was also a noted lumbering area with several sawmills, and it had two feed mills. The mill shown here was pulled down around 1991 and replaced with a parking lot and store.

It was built in 1890 on the site of an earlier mill that had burned. Considered quite modern at the time, in 1919 it merged with another company and became the Edmore Mill and Lumber Company. The mill was sold to Cargill Corporation in 1985.

I photographed the mill just a few days before demolition began. The owner had seen me taking pictures and asked if I would photograph the interior. I told him I would return the next day with lighting equipment, and he gave me a key and said I could help myself.

Most of the milling machinery was still in place. Though I am not superstitious in the least, I could sense the presence of the people who had labored there. Notes were penciled on the walls and the controls were in operating order. The day was rainy and cold. The photographs I made outside have a gloomy atmosphere, which mirrored my sense of loss when I thought of how near this venerable old place was to the end of it life.

This was a two-story mill with storage bins for grain on the second floor. It had three elevators with one serving another building that had been added around the early twentieth century. In fact, buildings were added from time to time, including shed structures to house the lumber. Like most mills, the basic structure was made of heavy timbers. The floors were thick to support the machinery and piles of feedbags. The mill must have processed a lot of beans because there were still piles of bags stenciled "Michigan Navy Beans" and "Edmore Grain and Lumber Co."

The ancient separator machinery was intriguing. All the operating parts were iron or steel set on a robust wooden frame. The faded labels were legible and indicated that the machines were built in Saginaw, Michigan. Edmore was served by two railroads—one was the Toledo, Saginaw and Muskegon Railroad—so the machines must have been delivered by that railroad. Most of the chutes were made of wood; the rest were metal. Everything had a texture that showed wear, but the machines were far from worn out and appeared ready to start running at any time. The mill's closing inconvenienced its customers. What had once been a local landmark and a place that hummed with activity was now gone.

This photo was made from just inside the front door, adjacent to the office. At the center are twin elevator shafts. Through the glass inspection window, three buckets of the elevator can be seen. At the left center are two chutes that funneled grain to grinding operations in the basement. At the far wall is a rack of shelving with spare parts for the various machines. The stairs lead to the second floor where the bins of stored grain are located. Note the "explosion-proof" light fixtures used throughout the mill.

The massive post and beam structure is evident here. The external shell of the building is much lighter—two by fours with sheathing and clapboards, like a typical house.

The grain separator in the Edmore mill was quite large for its time. A separator had three screens, each with different sized holes. The vibrating screens allowed field dirt and foreign materials to fall through two of the screens while the grain remained on the third screen. A strong air stream blew chaff and fine dirt off the grain.

The Fairbanks platform scale was almost a universal standard in feed mills, and remains so today. The feed products flowed down the wooden chutes and into bags.

In the distance, beyond one of the auxiliary buildings, is another feed mill that competed with Edmore Mill. It seems to have been a smaller operation.

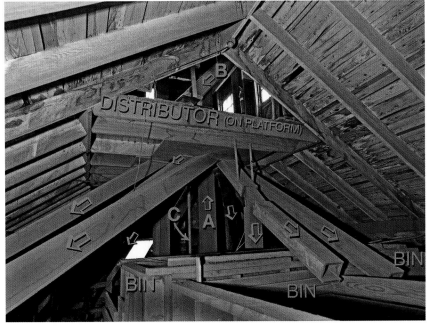

The distributor controls the direction of the flow of grain after the elevator has lifted it to the top of the mill. Later, more elevators were added, but they and their distributors were outside the mill, higher than the roof. Arrows indicate the direction of flow in the various chutes. The two distributor inputs are marked A and B. A is the elevator that brings the grain up from the lower level. B is a chute coming from another elevator outside the mill. The device shown in the photo (top) is the control for choosing which chute the grain will be directed to. The operator lifts the bar and moves it to one of the notches on the rim. The bar is dropped to rest in the chosen notch. Moving the bar rotates the shaft (labeled C), which turns a metal plate with a hole in it. When the hole is aligned with a chute, grain is conveyed to the desired bin.

STILL HERE . . . CEDAR SPRINGS MILL

According to the book, *The Cedar Springs Story*, by Sue A. Harrison and Donna J. DeJong (Cedar Springs Bicentennial Commission, 1976), Cedar Springs Mill was built in 1879 and purchased by Ernest Remer in 1886. It turned out to be a good buy. One year after his purchase, the mill shipped 150 traincar loads of potatoes, forty cars of hand-picked beans, twenty cars of wheat and rye, and 500 cars of hay. Remer also dealt in grains, sheep, wool, chickens, and probably fruit, as this is a fruit-growing region. When he died in 1931, his son Donald took over the operation. It was sold twice more and was taken over by current owner Sam Gebhardt in 1991.

Today the working mill is in fine condition. Its oldest section (framed above) is a wooden structure built with massive beams on a fieldstone foundation. There have been several additions and renovations through the years. The machinery varies in age from very old to modern and is updated from time to time. The oldest machines are a delight for the antiquarian, with wooden parts combined with heavy, cast iron components. They perform as well as anything made today.

The mill remains a vital part of its farming community because of its willingness to serve small-scale customers. It accepts small quantities of grain for milling and custom-grind feed mixes, working closely with its customers to meet their particular needs. Now we'll take a look inside.

Grain is brought to the mill by truck or in a grain trailer, sometimes called a gravity box.

When the trailer is parked over the loading bin, the door is opened and the grain flows into the bin and onto the elevator. Oats are being unloaded here.

These are the two elevators that lift the grain to the top of the mill. With the two inspection doors open, we can see the metal buckets attached to the rubber belts. When the buckets pass over the pulley at the top, they tip the grain into the distributor, which directs the grain into chutes that deliver it to the storage bins or machines. The operator uses the wheel to position the gate in the distributor.

Cedar Springs Mill offers customized services to its predominantly small- to medium-size customers. The farm and garden supplies store at the mill sells seed by the quarter-scoop or in 100-pound bags. The range of products is extensive. In addition to animal feeds, the mill sells grain seeds and grass seeds, including timothy and clover, in bag or bulk. They also stock a full range of fertilizers, pesticides, and herbicides, along with animal medicines and pet foods—products larger mills don't carry.

The grain is stored in bins on the second floor. It is delivered to processing stations on the main floor or to the mill in the basement through chutes that allow the grain to flow by gravity.

The chutes are constructed of wood, metal, and plastic. Wood is durable and easy to work with. The grain is quite abrasive, and the metal and plastic parts need to be replaced occasionally.

A separator (the folks at Cedar Springs call it the fanning machine) removes the foreign material that comes in with the grain—chaff, stems, small stones and so on. This machine is a Clipper Separator, made by the same company as the Ferrel separators.

The wooden chutes bringing grain from the storage bins on the floor above lead to a bagging station. Note the more modern metal chutes and flow controls, and also the heavy wooden posts and beams needed to support the great weight of the grain bins above.

The farm store stocks a large variety of pet and wild bird feeds. The sign on the office window announces the day when baby chickens, ducks, and turkeys will be available for sale. Children look forward to the event and are delighted by the little critters.

These are the two mixers, vertical on the left and horizontal on the right. The horizontal mixer is used most. Grain is loaded into the horizontal mixer by the auger conveyor, whose lower end passes through the floor grate to a bin in the basement. The horizontal mixer has paddles mounted to a motor-driven shaft. At the front of the mixer is the bag loader and scale.

A wheeled bin, or grain buggy, stands on the platform of a scale as grain is loaded from a chute delivering grain from a bin on the second floor. The ingredients in a mix are measured by weight.

The filled bin is wheeled to the grate near the mixer and the grain is released into the loading bin. The auger is started and the grain is conveyed into the horizontal mixer.

Some ingredients are put into the feed mix in liquid form. Molasses is pumped in through the pipes at left center. Molasses, and also added vegetable oil, contain some nutrients but their main contribution is to make the feed more palatable. Molasses also makes the feed sticky so that mineral ingredients remain equally distributed during transport.

Ropes passing through the ceiling are seen throughout the mill. They open the gates to the bins, allowing the grain to flow to the operations on the main floor. Like sailors, millhands have to "learn the ropes."

After being mixed, the feed is released into one of the bagging stations. The operator fits a bag over the openings in the chutes, then fills the bags with the mix. The bags usually hold 100 pounds of feed.

The hammermill (center of photo) is kept in the basement to isolate the building from the heavy vibrations and noise the mill produces. A hammermill is faster than a roller mill and produces finer textures. The "hammers" are rectangular steel plates that pivot on rods mounted on a revolving drum. The drum rotates at a high speed, causing the hammers to flail the grain to the selected coarseness. The milling machine, whether a hammermill or a roller mill, is far more efficient than the old millstones were. The air blower in the foreground is used to move the milled grain or waste materials such as corncobs.

Filled bags are brought to the dock for customer pickup.

The platform scale weighs incoming and outgoing loaded trucks and trailers. It is beside the office and store building.

Customers can view the scale from inside and outside the office window. Note the grain samples hanging from a shelf next to the scale.

The neighborhood as viewed from inside the mill. The white house is probably as old as the mill, as evidenced by its fieldstone foundation. The red building was once a stable.

At some point, the dock roof was reinforced with railroad rails. These were probably salvaged from repair work done on the mill's railroad siding.

Until about fifty years ago, Cedar Springs Mill had a competitor, Shaw's Mill, about a quarter-mile north. The building is now used as a manufacturing plant.

THE FUTURE . . . SIETSEMA FARMS MILL

Lake Montcalm Road isn't paved with yellow brick, but as you make your way on it you are surprised by an apparition that may put you in mind of Oz and the Emerald City. On a large, flat tract of land is a new feed milling operation, just twelve years old at the time of this writing. It is huge, and that alone impresses, but the impression grows when you tour the interior. The sense that we have left the present and moved into the future is almost eerie.

Eighteen stories tall and haloed by the sun, the mill is a scene for contemplation.

The milling facility is on the left, the truck station is at the center, with the storage bins and grain drier on the right.

The concrete silo is built into the corner of the milling tower. The tanks below contain liquid ingredients for the feed.

Viewed from the floor of one of the concrete silos, the concave floor above supports 900 tons of grain.

At the unloading station for trucks, incoming materials are placed on a drag conveyor. From there they are conveyed to either the storage bins shown here, or routed through the underground tunnel at the lower left corner. From there the materials will be transported to the concrete silos or commodity bins, depending on the product.

The drag conveyor emerges from the tunnel and loads incoming commodities into an elevator that moves it to the top of the milling tower.

The elevator carries the incoming commodities to the top of the milling tower and places it into the conical distributor. The distributor and other routing devices direct the commodities to one of sixteen destinations within the mill and the storage bins outside.

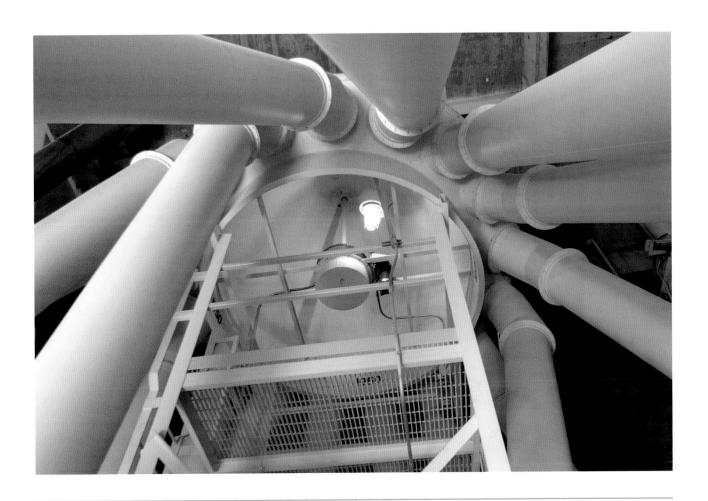

The distributor has a metal plate with a hole that can be positioned over any of the chutes. The electric motor rotates this plate on command from the control room on the ground floor of the milling tower.

Computer screens in the control room show the product level in each storage bin and the status of the many production operations. Most of the machines are directed from the control room, as is the flow of product from one station to another.

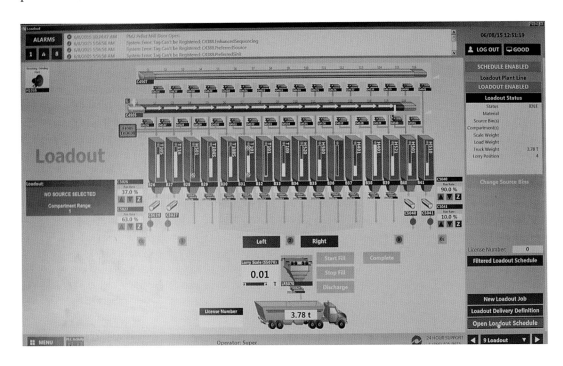

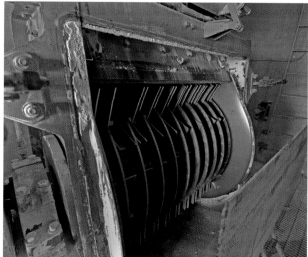

The hammermill can grind the incoming grain as fine as flour or into large particles, depending on whether the feed is intended for hogs or turkeys. Hammermills are capable of extremely high grinding speeds.

With the screen and cover door removed, the hammermill interior is revealed. Rectangular steel plates rotate on rods mounted on a spinning drum. The hammers flail the grain into small particles when the drum is spinning.

Stainless steel containers hold the dry additives that get mixed into the feed. Each recipe is based on the animal's age, size, and nutritional needs.

The mixer is the white, box-like structure on the floor. The ingredients are placed in the mixer through a large chute that releases product from two scales seen through the opening in the second floor. The mixtures may contain corn, wheat, soybean meal, vegetable oils, and other ingredients. All the products are formulated for animals raised in large numbers. The mixer shown here produces five-ton batches. The mill uses 50,000 pounds of recycled vegetable oil every day and three million bushels of corn per year. These numbers are strikingly large and suggest the enormous amount of food the farming industry is required to produce to meet the needs of 325 million Americans and many times that number of foreign customers.

After leaving the mixer, product is conveyed to the two pelletizers, one of which is shown here at the center rear of the photo. The cylinder above the pelletizer is the conditioner. It heats the product with steam to gelatinize the starches and adds special ingredients such as minerals before transferring it to the pelletizer.

The arrow on the pelletizing machine, with the door open, indicates the die through which the feed mix is extruded. The ingredients from the conditioner enter at the top and flow into a rotating chamber where the mix is forced through 26,000 holes in the die. As the die rotates, the formed pellets are sheared off by a stationary blade and drop into a chute in the floor.

After the pellets have passed through a cooler to bring them to ambient temperature, they are loaded into trucks for delivery to the farming operations with which Sietsema Farms contracts. Pelletizing the feeds assures that the ingredients are evenly distributed throughout the bulk and remain so during transport to their destination, which may be some distance from the mill. At the farm, the pellets are easier to handle than loose feed and are evenly distributed to the animals' feeding stations.

A retrospective view from the top of the milling tower takes in the countryside that provides raw ingredients for much of the mill's products. The maintenance crew has an even loftier view when performing maintenance atop the elevators.

Four
Mills
Reborn

IMPERIAL MILL

The Imperial Mill was established in 1868. Around 1970, it was purchased by a real estate developer who converted it into a spacious, beautiful home. The mill pond and its dam on Bear Creek was restored at the same time, when it was discovered that the water turbine that powered the mill's machines was intact and in good condition. The homeowner had the turbine restored to working order and coupled through a shaft to an electric generator inside the house. In addition to powering the house, current was fed into the local electrical grid. We know that other mills with turbines also installed generators and sold electricity to local residents during the hours the mill was not operating. The current owners may continue using the turbine to power to their home.

CEDAR SPRINGS MILL

Rockford is on the Rogue River. In 1844 the river was dammed, creating a large millpond. Mills and factories were built near the pond to take advantage of the water power. The Grand Rapids and Indiana Railroad tracks ran between the pond and the mills. When the railroad was abandoned, its roadbed was paved to create the White Pine Trail extending for ninety-two miles between Grand Rapids and Cadillac. A large park lies on both sides of the river, complete with a boat launch and a boardwalk meandering high above the river. Summer evenings often feature musical concerts in the park. The old mills have been converted into restaurants, stores, and ice cream shops. In fact, many old buildings around the dam are being reused, and the area has become a popular tourist attraction.

SHAW FEED MILL

The old photograph of the original Shaw Feed Mill was probably made between 1915 and 1920, judging by the automobiles and license plates. At some point, the mill's size was more than doubled, and a large rear addition was constructed around 1920. The mill competed with Cedar Springs Mill a quarter-mile away. Now the old building has been converted into a plant that produces industrial control panels. It has been insulated and has modern heating and air conditioning. Some of the old structure has been left exposed to good effect. The attic has not been changed and still contains the grain bins, wooden chutes, and distributor.

WATSON-HIGGINS MILLING CO.

The Watson-Higgins company produced flour and feed in Grand Rapids. In 1925 it added the building seen here, advertised as fireproof. Later, the wooden buildings were removed and the railroad tracks torn up. The office building survived and its renovations received a LEED Platinum rating for measures such as the use of recycled materials and low-water-use plantings. The area formerly occupied by the railroad tracks is now a rain garden, which collects storm water and slowly releases it into the ground rather than letting it run off the site and pollute waterways. Rainwater collected from the roof is used to irrigate the garden. The building is close to the center of Grand Rapids in a neighborhood that has seen extensive repurposing of old buildings, including vast furniture factories converted to office space, condominiums, and educational facilities. The entry walkway's bricks were salvaged after the street was repaved.

Gallery

This Portland mill was abandoned and ruined when local businessmen and brothers Charles and Edward Leik took it over. They restored the building to its original appearance, replicating the materials. Its thirty-foot by forty-foot footprint was typical of the times. Large wooden grain bins occupied the second story. The elevator rose beyond the roof and into a headhouse, which provided the height needed for the grain to flow into the bins. The filled bins weighed many tons, and the first-floor framing consisted of massive wooden posts and beams to support the weight. All the cleaning and some of the processing and routing of the grain was done on the first floor. The grinding machines were usually in the basement to isolate the rest of the mill from the noise and vibration they produced. Bagged feed was usually stored on the first floor, and subsequent additions provided more storage. Although the machinery is operational, the mill is used primarily for educational programs and functions as a community center. In its fully restored condition it presents an authentic view of how the early mills looked when they were new.

This old mill building in Ovid was photographed on a Sunday afternoon when no one could be found to provide information about it. It is certainly very old; the stone foundation suggests a date of around 1880. The large head-house and row of windows on the second floor hints that it may have originally been a flour mill. The absence of metal siding and the boarded windows indicate that it had been out of use for a long time, possibly serving as storage.

A mill in Lapeer wears its history in plain sight. It's an example of what might be called serial architecture. Additions were constructed through the years, and each one attached to a previous segment and all aligned with the railroad siding. The two-story structure in the foreground was probably the original building.

Newer grain bins from Michigan Agricultural Commodities in Middleton surround the original small elevator and mill.

A derelict mill in Fowler with its grain bins removed lends a melancholy mood to its town setting.

Then and now. This picture is emblematic of the ongoing history of country grain mills. The original mill still stands, while just down the road a newer and larger group of structures dominates the scene. The photograph was made in 1991 at Grand Ledge and the old mill was only a relic of its former economic importance.

A veritable castle in rural Michigan, the mill in Three Rivers was almost certainly the tallest building in the town.

In Reed City, the elevator nearly qualifies as a skyscraper. The pigeon population seems to prefer a lower altitude.

The Lawrence Roller Mill is in a state of near collapse. It was a water-powered mill standing next to its mill pond and the damp location may have undermined the foundation.

The Southwestern Michigan Feed Mill in Lawrence is a compact operation whose emphasis seems to be the farm supply store. The small greenhouse on the side is an unusual feature.

When a milling operation nears the end of its economic usefulness, it becomes a victim of deferred maintenance. Deterioration is inevitable and swift.

Ovid Farmers Elevator additions extended the original building along the railroad siding that served it. Each addition has its own headhouse for an elevator. A newer metal outside elevator sits on the opposite side of the building. The electric sign is an unexpected accessory.

A view of one of the Kellogg mills from the first floor, looking up at the bottom of the wooden grain bins, with their wedge shaped bottoms. The opening was connected to a chute with a gate that was opened by pulling on the wood handle, allowing grain to flow into the chute.

The little mill in Dorr was unchanged except for the addition of two outside storage bins. Its diminutive size probably reflected the size of its trading area. It was built on the edge of the town, which, in time, grew around it.

This empty parcel is the former site of the feed mill in Dorr. The old railroad station, once a companion to the mill, is at left. It is well cared for and awaiting transformation to another use.

The enormous collection of grain bins at Middleton are part of a business large enough to require product transport by train.

In Howard City, a venerable old mill is soon to be demolished.

The Howard City mill demolition reveals that the original wooden structure had later additions framed in steel.

The mill in Shepherd was originally owned by a business in Salt River. When Shepherd was platted west of Salt River, the railroad came to the new town, and several Salt River businesses, including the mill, moved there. Its history is on display at the railroad museum in the station, seen at the right. The elevator has been enlarged to its current commanding position along the railroad.

The mill at St. Johns is another example of a small mill that expanded along the railroad track.

The mill at Vermontville was once powered by a steam engine in the smaller attached building.

A thin blanket of snow reflects sunlight into the recesses of the mill in Woodland.

The Sunfield Elevator dominates the rural scene.

The mill in Sand Lake has a pleasing symmetry, no doubt unplanned by the builders.

The Sand Lake mill was closed and put up for sale in 2014. So far there have been no takers.

A casualty of Sand Lake mill's closing was the lighted Christmas star shining forth from the tallest structure in town. Other mills had similar stars, literally a highlight of the holiday season.

Two silos of the feed mill in Lowell form an imaginary gate in a castle.

The Coral Elevator is part of the picture on Main Street in Coral. After it closed, a collective of Amish farmers used it to store corn. They have since put it up for sale.

The Freeport mill appears to have a three-masted ship docked next to it, readying to sail across the amber waves of grain.

A gentle rhythm accentuates the roof lines of the mill at Lake Odessa.

The mill in Woodland on quiet and crisp winter's day, with a very old type of large trailer.

The mill cat in Fowler keeps a wary eye on the photographer. A light snow was falling, and the open door prompts a reminder that mills are unheated, and the work inside is sometimes done during periods of bitter cold.

The Comstock Park feed mill was shut down a short time before this photograph was made.

A trailer is loaded with grain at the Lawrence elevator. A grain trailer is commonly called a gravity box, because a hopper door at the bottom allows grain to flow out by gravity.

The last of winter's snow is melting into the ground, and the old mill in Woodland seems to be doing the same.

The mill in Westphalia has a rustic charm. Each mill has a stamp of originality and a distinct personality.

Westphalia Milling Company's faithful old truck brings a grain trailer into the mill.

The working Jones mill during a lull in business.

The corner of Main and Railroad Streets in Jones. The feed mill is a short walk up Railroad Street.

The Stanwood Farmer's Co-op mill is on Stanwood's main street.

It would be difficult to come up with more delightful feed mill ornament than the rooftop cornstalk that sprouted naturally at Stanwood.

The general store in Stanwood is just across the street from the feed mill.
Mill workers probably stopped by for snacks and cold drinks.

This building at Comstock Park mill had been empty for years. It was about the size of the earliest mills.

The Gibbard Brothers mill in Imlay City is built of "frostproof brick," an oversize brick with a smooth vitreous coating that repels water and provides some fire protection. This brick type is found on other building types, especially dairies.

Late-afternoon lull in Marne. The pile of material on the ground is probably lime.

The lyrics of an old song, "There's a tree in the meadow with a stream drifting by" seem to apply perfectly to this scene. The stream here is actually a drainage ditch, dug to remove excess water from the farm. Early settlers found good soil but also swamps, wetlands, lakes, rivers, and streams. Intensive work was required to establish well-drained land. Even with all these alterations, many wetlands remain, a haven for waterfowl, beavers, and other water-loving animals.

An auger drags grain from a bin and places it into a loading station, where conveyors will distribute it to production machinery or loading points.

A dam across Rogue River in Rockford provided power for several mills, including this one, which casts a perfect replica of itself on the calm millpond. The building was saved by being converted to a popular restaurant.

This mill, one of a group of three, is in Carson City. When it was built, around 1890, its elevator and grain storage bins were inside the building, as they were made largely of wood and had to be protected from the elements. The small added room on the rooftop is the headhouse, which accommodates the top of the elevator, providing the necessary height for distributing the grain. The tiny secondary room above the headhouse was probably added to increase the elevator height so that the grain could be sent to the building additions.

Six Lakes Elevator shows no signs of having had external elevators. All the grain storage bins must have been inside the building.

When the Six Lakes elevator closed, much of its machinery was removed. This old Ferrel separator was stripped of most of its metal parts, leaving the forlorn skeleton outside.

Demolition of one of the Kellogg Mills buildings provides an opportunity to study its construction. Despite the heavy timbers used in the internal framing, the exterior of the building was no stronger than that of an ordinary house, intended as only a shell to keep the weather off the framework and machinery. The shiplap siding, common on early mills, is revealed here because the metal siding that was added later has been removed as salvage. In time, all the mills came to be covered with some kind of metal siding. We can also see that building additions were merely tacked on to the original structure instead of extending it.

The Kellogg mill has massive timber framing.

It is tempting to refer to the second-floor protrusion as "Juliet's Balcony." In fact, it's a ventilation stack and extended down to the bottom of the panel on the side of the building. The two hooded openings directed chaff and dirt generated by the grain separator downward. The fine dust exits through the openings near the roof.

The mill in Bangor is decorated for the holidays with a greeting
spelled out in lights above the porch at the entrance.

The ancient Fairbanks scale is still in use at Bangor. The metal grain scoops resting on the top of the scale are used for adding or removing small quantities of product to bring a sack to its proper weight. The scoop design hasn't changed in hundreds of years.

The truck loading station at Conklin.

When the Conklin mill closes down for the day, the local
pigeons and squirrels move in to clean up the spillage.

The Kent City mill once extended some distance along the railroad track. Today this is an open tract of land save for a new farm supply store. The railroad is still operating.

On a hot summer Sunday afternoon, the Kent City mill crew and their families are likely cooling off at a nearby lake.

Everything at Kent City bespeaks the mill's advanced age. The old dock roof was still in place even though a new enclosure had been built around it.

The Sparta mill sits on the banks of Nash Creek. The building shown here was built in 1952 after a fire destroyed the original, late-1800s mill. Parts of the old structure are incorporated in the present building.

The mill buildings in Lake Odessa straddled the railroad siding; train cars
were loaded by chutes that overhung the track.

They really mean it . . . smoking in a mill is decried by everyone, even smokers. Even the electric lights are "explosion proof" with the bulbs enclosed in a Pyrex hood.

This desolate scene at a mill undergoing demolition in Lawrence evokes the end of an era in American agriculture.

In the 1950s, this Grand Trunk Western freight train pulled into the mill district in Coopersville. The mill at the left of the track closed recently, and the principal mill buildings on the right have been replaced by a modern store. The tracks are still in place and used by a tourist railroad.

This small, shuttered mill in Burnips never outgrew its original size.
A nearby church converted the building into a youth activity center.

Notes tacked to the
door of the Burnips
mill instruct
customers to take
their business to the
mill in Dorr. After
that mill closed, too,
farmers had to travel
even farther for grain
services.

When the mill in Burnips shut down, it left a hole in this small-town economy. When farmers brought their produce to the mill, they would also do some shopping. There was likely a link between the mill shutdown and the closing of Teed's market.

The Big Rapids mill has been freshened up with metal siding and significantly enlarged through the years. It still retains its long cupola and foursquare headhouse even though a modern elevator towers over the building. The mill now bills itself as a farm and garden supply business to attract gardeners as well as farmers.

The Amish-run Maple Valley mill is about size of regional mills of the late 1800s. However, this is a modern building with modern equipment serving a small but dedicated clientele.

The New Era mill's scale office is quiet on a hot midsummer day.

Mills displayed a multitude of metal advertising signs, and the rusted nail holes left in this New Era mill door demonstrate how many signs have decorated it over the years.

Photographed in 1995, the mill at New Era embodies rural rustic charm.

The New Era mill's authentic characteristics include a blackboard posted outside the building to display current prices. In 1904, the trade press hotly debated whether this practice was useful and appropriate.

Harvey's feed mill in Carson City started life in 1880 as a flour mill. The shed-roof addition at far left covers the pit that held the water turbine that powered the mill. The turbine was still in use in the late 1940s, though only in combination with electric motor power. The turbine is still in place and the mill pond that powered it is much smaller.

This dam on Fish Creek powered Harvey's Mill. The wooden boards that were raised and lowered to control the level of the millpond have been removed, leaving only the concrete base of the dam. A footbridge has been installed along the top.

This old mill was said to be the last feed mill in Grand Rapids. It was probably built in the 1880s and later survived by selling building materials, pet foods, and garden supplies. Today, a group of stores occupies the land the mill stood on.

Rolling terrain typically surrounds old mills, and scattered woodlots bordering the farms are still prevalent.

The mill in Grant is ancient. There is evidence that the foundation was once raised, perhaps to provide a basement to house milling equipment.

The platform scale at the Grant mill is ancient. Fairbanks scales were used almost exclusively in the area; they were built to last, and they all have. Nearly all mills placed the balance in a bay window next to the scale, allowing it to be read by both the workers inside the mill and the customer outside.

Long before green roofs became a trend, the mill in Grant was regularly sprouting a crop, thanks to the combined effects of spillage and wind.

This scene in Grant presented itself as a composed medley of textures and rhythm.

In the 1800s, cedar shingles were an important manufactured product in this area. They could last a long time, as the shingles on the Grant mill testify. The rusted metal sign and weathered shingles seem to merge.

This beautiful brass machine in the Ithaca mill office is not a still or espresso machine. It is a seed divider, or seed sorter. Seeds are fed into the funnel and fall into sieves with thirty-eight different sizes of holes. This sorts the seeds and directs them to the discharge chutes at the bottom. Known as the Boerner type of seed sorter, it is still being made of brass, and hand assembled. Modern machines use electricity and centrifugal force to sort seeds.

Ithaca's mill district once included four mills clustered near the railroad track. Two of the current mills are devoted to bean production. This distinctive, two-story brick building is part of the mill that handles soybeans. The second floor was formerly used for "bean picking," where workers, usually girls or young women, could find seasonal work. They sat at a row of bean picking machines, removing those that were discolored or malformed. The row of windows provided natural light. Today, machines do the sorting work in the bean plant across the street. The brick building dates from 1898 and houses the offices.

An old bean picking machine sits in the office. The worker would sit on a stool or chair with her feet on the treadle. The treadle rotated the flywheel, which drove the conveyor belt at the top of the machine. Beans were poured into the metal hopper and the conveyor belt would deliver them to the sorter, who put the rejected beans into trays on the left and right of the belt. The marketable beans fell off the end of the belt onto the inclined trough and then into a basket or pail. From there they would be carried to a bagging operation. Rejected beans were probably used as animal feed.

The mill in Saranac is unusual because it loads grain into trucks parked at the curb on a town street. There's no doubt that the mill deals in Purina products.

It's harvest time, and the mill at Lapeer is staying open late to accommodate the line of trucks and trailers waiting to unload grain.

A truck hoist at a mill in Ovid. The sail-like boom and tarpaulin
mounted on the hoist rail is something of a mystery.

The Farmers Co-op in Zeeland is built of frostproof glazed brick, an extraordinarily substantial material. The business has grown considerably since this photo was made.

Sometimes small mills grow into large ones. Since the photo at the top was made, the Zeeland Farmers Co-op has grown mightily to become one of the largest soybean processors in the US (above).

A diesel locomotive, which once shunted cars around on the tracks at the Kellogg mills, is slowly being engulfed by vines.

At the Kellogg mills, the railroad has been abandoned and the rails taken up. This section remains as part of the private Sweetline railroad consisting of seven miles of track between Carson City and Middleton.

The distinctive Purina checkerboard emblem is ubiquitous in farm country. Here it graces the mill in Coopersville.

The mill in North Star had ceased operating five years before this photo was made. There are dozens of wind-driven electricity generators in the area. They were installed after the mill shut down, and it is ironic to reflect that if the mill had continued operating, it would be powered by a windmill.

Hastings has both a Mill Street and a Railroad Street, which makes the mill particularly easy to find.

This small mill serves White Cloud. The basic structure is patterned after a barn, with a small brick rear addition. The pile of dark material at lower left is coal; mill operators were always seeking additions to their business.

The White Cloud mill contains a wonderful panoply of siding materials, including brick, board and batten, shiplap, clapboard, corrugated metal, tar paper, and even a license plate used as a patch.

The elevator at the rear of the White Cloud mill is very small and might be an auxiliary to a larger one inside the building. The headhouse is certainly large enough to contain a substantial elevator.

The White Cloud mill sports the typical collage of metal signs and a blackboard posting commodity prices.

On a warm, sultry autumn evening in St. Johns, the mill is working late to keep up with the harvest.

Hamilton is home to one of the largest soybean processors in the country.

A hand-operated grain cleaning machine, sometimes called a separator or fanning machine, removes chaff and field dirt from the grain. The trademark is illegible but this may be a Clipper product. The drum reads "over 15,000 in use."

The grain cleaning machine contains three mesh screens used interchangeably to accommodate different kinds of grain.

The bulletin board at Tom's Mill in Coopersville is a convenient place to offer horses, goats, ducks, and burritos for sale.

The bagging station at Walcott's mill in Allendale.

Located next to the Grand River in Portland, the ADM Animal Nutrition plant can be included in the mills denoted as "modern" since it dates from some time after the 1930s.

The mill at Vestaburg has been out of operation for years, but the property is well kept, perhaps implying a future restart. The Heartland bicycle trail, utilizing an old railroad grade, is at far right.

The mill and elevator in Charlotte is one of four operated by the Eaton Farm Bureau Co-Op. The photograph incorporates the three elements we expect to see in traditional settings; the time-honored mill, the railroad and a charming and substantial railroad station. We can only guess at the contents of the tank car which might be molasses or liquid fertilizer.

This photograph at the Caledonia Farmers Elevator was made
thirty years ago when the railroad still passed through the facility.
The train station is to the right.

A recent picture of the Caledonia operation shows many changes, although the basic layout remains. The tracks are gone, but the train station provides storage for the mill's products.

This building at the Caledonia elevator is quite old and was built as a flour mill.

The updated Caledonia building is now used as a cattle feed mill.

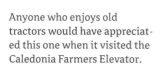
"Built By George Staiger Oct 10 - 1915"

The main mill building at Caledonia uses the original scale hopper. A penciled notation on the side of the hopper was written by a Mr. Staiger in 1915, the year the mill was built. The year 2015 marked its 100th anniversary, an event celebrated in Caledonia.

Anyone who enjoys old tractors would have appreciated this one when it visited the Caledonia Farmers Elevator.

This control regulates the flow of grain from storage to production. Turning the lever rotates a pulley in back of the disc, which moves the cables seen at the top of the picture. The cables rotate the distributor cone to direct the grain into the desired chute.

Notes like this one can be found in all mills. They remind the workers how to deal with a stubborn piece of equipment. They may also spell out the order in which operations should be performed. The metal handles on the cables are an example of adaptive reuse, made of worn-out hammers from the hammermill.

Ingredients for a feed mix are measured and brought to this point to be loaded onto the concave conveyor belt that will transport them to the mixer. Note that there are loading points along the length of the conveyor. Small quantities of supplements are weighed out and added by hand. The mixer is just beyond the opening in the far wall.

Mill workers must negotiate catwalks and ladders to service the machinery.

Loading docks take a heavy beating, and this venerable specimen
at Fowler shows evidence of long use.

This modern bagging station eases the burden of moving 100-pound bags through the filling operation.

The Caledonia Farmers Elevator is a study in grays and perspective.

At this abandoned mill in Vickeryville, one of the two exterior grain bins has been removed, along with much of the machinery. The mill is reputed to be haunted, a dubious proposition unless an occupation by raccoons is considered a form of haunting.

At the Alto Farm Services mill, a truck hoist is used to tip trucks to unload their grain.

The mill in Alto was once the largest complex of buildings in the small town. Now all that remains is the concrete footprint of the main building and three concrete silos.

A truck waits in the loading bay in Alto. The large silo and two
adjacent concrete silos are vestiges of this once sizable operation.

The scale building and two bins at Alto.

At Moline, the co-op elevator is situated on both sides of a street,
an unusual arrangement.

A vertical mixer and ancillary equipment dominate the interior of
a modern mill in Caledonia.

After a heavy run of the grinding equipment, a worker remarked, "The place looks like a Halloween haunted house." Fine dust and static electricity quickly builds the network of cobwebs. Cleaning it requires diligent work with brooms and shovels.

A rear view of the two bean elevators in Ithaca. The one on the right is for soybeans; the other is for navy, black, pinto and other beans typically sold whole. These are sometimes called "white" beans, and it is interesting to note that they are all varieties of the same plant.

Another view of the oldest mill building at Caledonia

Flour mills look different from feed mills. Shown here is the flour mill at Dowagiac.

Nothing evokes loneliness more than an uninhabited mill. When the wind blows, the elevators moan and sigh, just like on a ship.

Sunlight takes the deep textures of a shut down mill in Lowell.

It's hard to say which building at St. Johns is more handsome—
the mill or the railroad station.

The station at St. Johns sits in a parklike setting. There's no doubt that the townspeople appreciate their old building.

A cluster of mill buildings in Shepherd.

Another example of objects that have arranged themselves in a graceful, even balletic, position.

The decaying mill in Vickeryville, primarily a bean operation, was one of three owned by Francis Rockafel-low. The other two were in Carson City and Vestaburgh.

The flour mill at Hart was a roller mill and may have also produced animal feed. The exposed chains and sprockets would not be code-compliant today. The large pulley carried a belt from a lineshaft near the ceiling to deliver power to this machine.

A Howes flour packing machine at the Hart mill. A flour sack was placed on the stand under the filling pipe. Flour flowed from the pipe into the sack. The stand could be raised or lowered by the wheel on its right side. Two elevators, one on each side of the machine, are enclosed in wood covers with oval glass inspection windows. The three ropes on the elevator at the right controlled the gates that directed grain throughout the operation.

The grain cleaner at the Hart mill, most likely a Clipper model, separates the incoming grain from foreign materials, such as field dirt, chaff, small stones, and weed seeds. The dirt is blown out of the machine by the fans at the top. Cleaned grain falls from the bottom and into a bin for transport through the mill.

Another view of the separator in Hart. The pulleys held the leather belts that powered the machine. The drawers on the front held the screens that were vibrated to separate the materials fed into the cleaner. Although wood is the dominant material, it has a cast iron frame for the machine parts.

The scale at Hart is obviously very old. The wooden box behind the old scale at Hart is the hopper. A feed recipe's ingredients are loaded into the hopper. The load is weighed after every addition to assure the correct proportion of ingredients.

Trufant calls itself the "stump fence capitol of the USA." So it is appropriate that this stump puller, invented by a local farmer, is featured on the village green, with County Line Farms mill in the background. Pine stumps have long been used as a garden ornament in Trufant, and cattle fences made of the stumps are a common sight. Even the post office has a few stumps in its landscape.

Grain bins were almost always on the second floor of the mill building, but at the Trufant mill, the tapered bottoms penetrate the first floor, at the right height for loading the rail cars that stood behind the building. Two by four boards were stacked and nailed in an offset pattern to create the taper.

It is amazing how long the machinery can be kept working. Trufant's separator and scale hopper are still in perfect working condition.

This is the oldest elevator at County Line Farms, with its cover removed. The opening was for loading from the first floor, but most loading was done from the bin in the basement. A penciled note on the leg reads, "Belt replaced July 23, 1943." The elevator was probably installed when the mill was built in the 1880s.

The mixer's ingredients are emptied into a bin; an auger conveyor will lift it into a waiting truck.

An old Ford tractor and grain trailer wait in the unloading area.

Small but sturdily built with large bricks, the mill at Overisel is basic and petite.

This photograph contains clues about the history of the Shaw Mill in Cedar Springs. At lower right, the elevator's wood legs have been removed to expose the pulling and tensioning device. The wooden bin with the sloping bottom fed grain into the elevator. The chute passing through the wall behind the elevator carried coal to the floor below the bin. Some of the loading bin framing shows scorch marks, probably lumber reused after a fire. The concrete base under the vertical beam and the concrete bolster under the stone, at left, suggests that the town has many springs and many buildings have problems with water in their basements.

The old mill in Coopersville reminds us of the Gilbert and Sullivan lyric which sings of "a thing of parts and patches." It is obviously on the last leg of its existence. Still, the mill cat rests easily on the roof near the chimney.

The combination feed mill/lumber company is common. They have little affinity except for their location next to the railroad track. Workers may have moved between the two seasonal businesses.

At Harvey's Mill in Carson City, the corn sheller stripped corn off the cobs. The kernels were then cracked or ground.

Cobs are usually removed from the mill by a blower, which piles them up outside. They are free for the taking and sometimes used as animal bedding. In the past, the cobs mixed with sawdust were used to insulate ice houses.

Conklin was once on a branch line of the Grand Rapids and Indiana railroad, now a bicycle trail.

Conklin's Main Street is divided into two parts with commercial buildings and a post office on one side and a mill on the other. This one-block commercial district hosts the world's shortest St. Patrick's Day parade. A high school band and revelers gather at one end of the street and parade to the opposite end, where they pile into the Fenian Pub.

The mill owns one side of Main Street in Conklin.

It's a cold day, and the grain drier at the mill in Fowler is emitting clouds of vapor. Grain's moisture content must be below fifteen percent or it will clog machinery and rot in storage. The grain moves through the chutes with a rattling, hissing sound that lets folks know the mill is operating.

The mill in Vriesland, viewed across a meadow.

A Clipper grain cleaner of recent vintage.

Feed mills through the country have the same general outline,
as shown in this comparative photo of a mill in Missouri.

On a summer day in a mill town, kids will gather at the grocery store for ice cream or cold drinks. Unfortunately, the store in Cloverdale is closed, but the kids still congregate here.

Most of the mill trains have left the station for good. A caboose is on display near the Ravenna feed mill. The track is now a bicycle path.

When a building achieves a certain age, it shows the history of wear and tear caused by weathering and hard use. This is certainly on display at the loading dock of the ancient mill in Grant.

After the mill in Lakeview suffered a serious fire thirty-five years ago, milling operations were suspended and the facility continued operating as an elevator only. It now includes a modern farm supply store across the street, along with a large lawn and garden store. The small white building at the far left is the original train station, now renovated and used to store fertilizer, seeds, and other products sold at the elevator.

The North Central Co-op in Fremont is a large milling and elevator operation. It uses the railroad and a fleet of trucks to transport the production volume.

Most of the metal siding has been removed for salvage from the mill in Bellevue, revealing the original wood, painted barn red. The mill is shut down, as are an office and scale building across the street.

The North Central Co-op plant is on a busy street in Fremont, so this grand mural is in a high-visibility location where it can be appreciated by passersby. The mural's agricultural theme is executed in a faux primitive style that matches the age and character of the operation. The legend panel at the right depicts a capsule history of the business.

Ferrel grain cleaning machines are found in nearly all mills, regardless of the mill's age. They were also sold under the Clipper trademark and varied in size from small ones equipped with wheels that allowed them to be moved around and powered by a hand crank, to this large one in the elevator at Lakeview. Their design and basic wood construction continued until at least 1980, when they evolved to an all-metal design. There are companies who rebuild even very old machines to like-new condition and sell them around the world. Depending on the region, they are called grain cleaners, separators, or fanning machines.

The End. *Photo by Glenn Holley, 1970.* Courtesy of Eaton Farm Bureau Co-Op.

More
About
Mills

An early wagon hoist appears to be operated by a ratchet jack.

This unloading station in Moline has a truck hoist, used to unload trucks that don't have tilting beds. The rear of a truckbed loaded with grain is positioned over the unloading bin (E). The truck's front wheels are positioned over the hoist platform (D). The cable hooks (C) are engaged with triangular steel clips at the sides of the hoist platform. The hoisting winch (A) is activated to raise the front of the truck and tip the grain into the loading bin. The hoisting mechanism is on a wheeled frame that can move along the track (B) and be positioned to accommodate trucks of various lengths.

The term gristmill is found in old references to what we would call a flour mill or feed mill. The word grist derives from Middle English and refers to any grain that is ground and used as a food. The term is now considered archaic. Before about 1850, mills typically used millstones, or stone grinding wheels. The newer roller mills and hammer mills work faster, need less power, are easier to adjust for particle size, and don't introduce stone dust into the product.

One of a pair of millstones on display at the Oakfield Historical Museum. They were removed from a local mill, since demolished.

In contrast to feed mills, flour mills produce meal almost exclusively for human consumption. In the second half of the nineteenth century, millers developed methods of processing grain that removed the germ from the wheat seeds and the outer shell, or bran, before the final grinding. This makes the flour white and produces bread with a light, airy consistency. If the germ and bran are removed before grinding, they may later be reintroduced into the flour. The resulting combination is called whole wheat flour and is a light brown color. Incidentally, farm animals were always fed whole grains. Today, nutritionists suggest avoiding white refined flour, but in the nineteenth century, millers advertised their white flour as being more nutritious than whole wheat. White flour cost more and was associated with wealthy households, whereas whole wheat was for the poor. The ad for white flour from Valley City Milling Co. makes a subtle reference to royalty, perhaps suggesting a class distinction.

Flour mills and feed mills were almost always separate businesses, though some mills produced both products. Feed mill products were mostly distributed locally, while flour mills usually had a much larger market base.

Advertisement in the *Grand Rapids Herald* in 1897 for white refined flour.

196

ANIMAL FEED

Feed mills produce food for cattle, hogs, sheep, goats, dogs, cats, poultry, and fish. There are specific recipes for each animal subgroup, and special formulations within each subgroup. For example, different blends are targeted for pregnant animals and those who have digestive or growth problems or other ailments. If you visit a feed mill you will see its storage area filled with bags of special blends. The well-known Purina company was an early producer of specialized feed blends, which they sold as "chows."

Although farmers have known for centuries that an animal's diet can affect its health, scientific studies weren't conducted until the nineteenth century. Growing knowledge about vitamins and minerals led to the formulation of specific feeds. There are two broad categories of animal feeds—those for animals that are polygastric, meaning that they have stomachs with more than one compartment, as do cattle sheep and goats. Pigs, horses, poultry and fish are monogastric. They get along with a stomach that has one compartment. Feed recipes take this into account.

Cows can get all their nutritional needs from eating grass. But this applies to fresh, green grass. Toward the end of the growing season, grass becomes dried and loses some nutritional value. Farmers cut and dry hay as a means of preserving it, but hay will only get animals through the winter. So farmers use supplementary feeds to keep their animals healthy.

Hogs are different. According to Kevin Turner of the Swine Research Department at Michigan State University, hogs will eat almost anything and thrive. If a hog has a finicky appetite, Turner tells us, adding something sweet to its food will quickly solve the problem. There was a time when American towns and cities had "piggeries." A hog farm would be established on the outskirts of the town and the farmer who ran it collected the town's garbage, which he fed to the hogs. This quaint custom was discontinued when townsfolk started including trash in their garbage.

Farm animals are prone to ingesting parasites and other organisms that can sicken them. Medicinal products are often included in their feed. To prevent overeating, fillers such as spent distillery mash, beet trimmings, and other items are added.

FIT FOR A PIG

A typical mix for hog feed is seventy to seventy-five percent corn, twenty-five percent soybeans, and trace minerals, vitamins, and salt. Sometimes fillers are substituted for some of the ingredients. These include beet residue from sugar mills, spent distillery mash, fruit rejects, and so on. Whatever the basic recipe, it is modified to reflect the hogs' size, age, and condition.

In addition to feeds, fertilizer, pesticides, herbicides, lime, poultry grit, and of course, seeds, mills often carry hardware items such as fencing, water tanks, and other farm supplies. In the past they also sold coal, drain tiles, and even lumber to smooth out seasonal business.

MACHINERY

Elevator. All mills use an elevator, or conveyor, to move grain to the highest point in the mill so that it can be released through chutes that direct the grain to different destinations. Without an elevator, in former times, grain would be carried through the mill in pails and tubs, which was backbreaking work. Mechanical elevators eliminated most of the onerous lifting.

Oliver Evans, an American inventor, designed the bucket elevator and patented it in 1787, one of the earliest patents granted by the US Patent Office. Evans's ingenuity lay in observing that grain can flow like water under the influence of gravity. He employed his bucket elevator to "pump" the grain to a height above the mill and then let it flow through pipes, or chutes, with a system of gates to control distribution. Evans simultaneously used his new invention as the basis of an entire automated system of grain handling in a mill. All feed mills have elevators, but they also *are* elevators, hence the building term grain elevator.

The terms "mill" and "elevator" are often used interchangeably. That's because a mill receives grain and then processes it, principally by grinding. The elevator receives grain and stores it before shipping it out to another location, which may be a mill. The farmer's use of one term or the other would be dictated by how he used the facility. If he brought grain to be milled, he would call it a mill. If he was simply selling the grain, he might say he was taking it to the elevator. Historically, some mills became principally elevators and some elevators did some milling. No one would fault a visitor for using either term. The term elevator typically describes both a type of business and the machine—a vertical conveyor used to move grain through both mills and elevators.

Chutes carry the grain to storage containers, called bins. A bin is a more recent version of the silo and differs mainly in being constructed of steel rather than concrete, usually corrugated steel. Grain bins are usually larger than silos and may contain electronic sensors to measure heat, and heaters to prevent grain from freezing.

Older, smaller mills had wood storage bins on the second floor. If the mill grew and required more storage capacity, it would add bins outside the mill building, usually made of corrugated metal but sometimes of concrete.

The bottoms of these bins are shaped like inverted cones to direct the grain into a gated chute attached to the bottom of the bin. When the gates are opened the stored grain flows to the areas where processing is done.

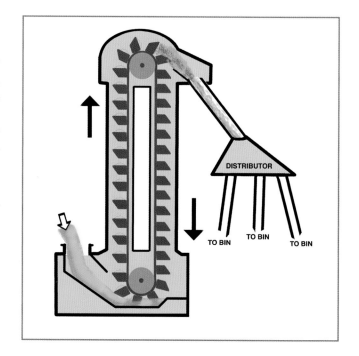

Grain brought to the mill is unloaded into a bin located just below ground level. This unloading bin has a slanted bottom, causing the grain to flow to the bottom of the bucket elevator. The elevator belt moves continuously, with the buckets scooping up the grain. When the buckets reach the top of the elevator, they tip and centrifugal force flings the grain into a chute that carries it to the distributor. The distributor has a metal plate that stops the grain from flowing into the chutes. The plate has a single hole that is rotated to line up with one of the chutes. The grain is thus directed to the desired bin. The rotating plate is controlled at the bottom of the elevator by an operator using cables or a rotating metal shaft. At larger operations, the plate is rotated by a motor controlled by electric switches.

Elevators are just one of the types of conveyors used. Another common one is the auger conveyor. It is used to move grain from one bin to another, to bring grain from a bin and into the mill, and to load grain into the grinding machines and mixers. It is also used to load and unload trucks. The auger has a rotating screw inside a close-fitting tube. The screw is turned by a motor.

A drag conveyor moves materials in greater volume and speed than the auger conveyor. It resembles an elevator that has been laid on its side. Drag conveyors are often used to move products over long distances.

Grinding. The invention of the roller mill was responsible for the demise of millstones. Roller mills are smaller and lighter than the stones, easier to adjust for particle size and much faster in operation. In its simplest form, a roller mill has two metal rollers about a foot in diameter with their surfaces engraved with sharp-edged grooves. The two rollers are mounted facing each other and are rotated in opposite directions. Grain flows into the space between the rollers, which pinch the grain as it is driven past them. The grinding is done by the cutting edges of the grooves. The space between the rollers can be adjusted to control coarseness. The ground grain drops into a bin and then onto a conveyor that carries it to a bagging operation or to another step in the production. Modern mills typically use two pairs of rollers, and sometimes three. The first pair produces a coarse grind and the grain drops to the next pair of rollers, grinding it to a finer texture.

This type of roller mill is found in a large, modern mill. It has two pairs of rollers like those shown in the diagram. One of the photographs shows a mill with the cover removed, revealing one of the rollers. All four rollers have fine grooves with sharp edges that cut and grind the grain to a fine consistency.

Hammermill

View inside the hammermill

Hammermills were developed after roller mills. They are faster and capable of producing a much smaller particle, but they produce more dust and require more power to operate. The "hammers" are steel plates about four by ten inches and about three-eighths-inch thick. Each plate has a hole at one end and the plates are fitted on steel axles mounted around a drum. The hammers rotate freely on the axles. The drum rotates at high speed, which causes the hammers to stand out from the drum through centrifugal force. They literally hammer the grain into particles. An additional advantage of hammermills is that they can be used when the grain has a relatively high moisture content.

A modern mill may have both a roller mill and a hammermill. The choice of which type to use is based on desired particle size and grain type or condition.

Mixer

Grain dryer

Mixing. The mixer is one of the principal machines in a mill. It consists of a cylinder with rotating paddles on a shaft turned by a motor. The ingredients of a feed recipe are conveyed into the mixer, which combines them into a uniform mixture. During the mixing process, additional dry or liquid ingredients such as minerals, vitamins, medications, and digestive aids may be added. Mixers vary greatly in size depending on the mill's capacity.

A feed mill may have a grain dryer to dry incoming grain to a moisture content of less than fifteen percent. Some mills require incoming product to already be dried to this standard. A higher moisture content can clog the machinery and cause stored products to spoil.

Scales. Every feed mill has several scales. The scales can be divided into two types: the large platform scale located outside the mill, used to weigh loaded incoming and outgoing trucks or trailers, and smaller scales inside the mill to apportion the quantities in a feed recipe and to weigh the products when they are sold. Platform scales are set flush with the ground and are often large enough to accommodate a tractor-trailer.

Power. Despite the prevalence of rivers and streams in the southern part of Michigan's Lower Peninsula, I could not find evidence of a single mill powered by the large, picturesque water wheels we see in old paintings. That's probably because feed mills weren't prevalent here until after the Civil War, when other power options became available. Before that, the farming community wasn't very large and most farms were subsistence operations, with grain production done manually at the farm.

Early mills had three options for powering their machinery: water, steam, and animals. Steam power was easy to harness, and it meant that a mill didn't have to be close to a source of water power. Steam engines required fuel, either wood or coal.

Water power was an excellent choice, too, but only for mills near a reliable source of moving water. Given this part of the state's rolling terrain, a stream or river would need to be dammed to provide a head of water of at least eight feet. If this could be arranged, then the mill could make use of the water turbine, developed for use in American mills in the late 1850s.

Hagood Mill in South Carolina.
The waterwheel is the "overshot" type.
Water was carried to it by a flume upstream from the mill.

Compared to the old-fashioned and somewhat delicate wooden water wheels, the turbine was compact, about three or four feet in diameter and three to six feet tall. Its basic form is quite simple. There is a circular iron or bronze cylinder with a rotating shaft through its center. Attached to this shaft are a number of paddles, called vanes. Under pressure from the dam, water is forced into the housing and against the vanes. This turns the shaft and the gear that connects the shaft to the mill's machinery. The tall shaft reached above the water level and a crown gear turned a horizontal shaft that led into the mill and drove the machinery. Refinements in the design made it possible to maximize the energy of the flowing water. Efficiency can be close to ninety percent. The energy is clean, and best of all, free. Maintenance usually involved removing debris consisting of sticks or leaves and adjusting the water lever in the mill pond.

A prime advantage of the water turbine is that its operating speed and power can be easily adjusted. In the earliest turbines, the vanes were fixed rigidly to the power shaft. Later improvements allowed operators to adjust the angle of the vanes, and thus the speed and power could be regulated from inside the mill. Because of these efficiencies, mills quickly adopted the turbine, and over time, some mills hooked up an electric generator to the turbine so that at night, when the mill was shut down, it could generate electric power and the power could be sold to the neighborhood.

Electricity powers today's mills. Perhaps its biggest advantage was the elimination of the lineshaft, a large shaft that ran through the mill and was rotated by the turbine or steam engine.

A machine shop powered by line shafts and belts.

The shaft had a number of pulleys, one for each machine that had to be powered. The power from the shaft was transmitted to the pulley on a machine by a leather belt. To start a machine, a lever was pulled that moved an idler pulley to tighten the leather belt on the pulleys. To stop the machine, the idler pulley was backed off, which released the tension on the belt, allowing it to slip on the pulleys. Powering all the machines from a single power source presented a considerable danger to the workers. All those belts flailing away caused many severe accidents and even fatalities. The dangers weren't confined to grain mills. Most factories were powered in the same way. Another big problem was the belts, which were prone to wear and breakage. The belts consisted of several plies of leather glued together and were three to twelve inches wide. If a belt broke or was damaged, a skilled "belt splicer" had to be called in to make the repair.

The electric motor allowed for distributed power. Each machine could be powered by its own motor that was easy to start and stop. The motor could be sized for the machine it drove. The increase in worker safety was immense, and the number of crippling accidents plummeted.

Early on, electricity's limiting factor was availability. In some rural locations, electric power didn't become available until the late 1930s. Even then, it took the formation of a government agency, the Rural Electrification Administration, to advance the supply of electricity into rural America. Before that time, power companies were reluctant to bear the expense of stringing wire and building substations when the scarcity of customers meant that it took a long time for the expense to be recouped. In some places, rural cooperatives and towns built their own generation plants to bypass the power companies. Today, only museum mills use water or steam power.

FORM FOLLOWS FUNCTION

If you look at pictures of old mills, you'll notice that in the nineteenth and early twentieth centuries, mills were much smaller than they were in, say, 1940 or 1950. Expansion came during WWI in 1917–18, when the US government passed measures encouraging farmers to increase production by increasing the number of acres under cultivation. The best-known example occurred when farmers in Oklahoma and other states were encouraged to plant cotton for use in military uniforms, tents, and tarpaulins, even though the climate and soils were unsuitable. Farmers also produced bumper food crops to feed the military and prospered accordingly. When the armistice ended the war, the country found itself with surplus foodstuffs. Farmers were caught in a squeeze with produce that they could sell only at reduced prices while the cost of living was going up. Then came a recession in 1920 and 1921 that hit the agricultural community hard. Farmers destroyed some of their crops to drive prices up, resulting in public outrage. Blame was passed around and the mill owners were caught in the middle. The farming community did not fully recover until the late 1930s and the start of WWII.

Another characteristic of older mills is the cupola, or headhouse. This housed the part of the elevator that projected above the roof. Early elevators were built mostly of wood and needed protection from the weather, and the leather belts to which the buckets were attached deteriorated if they got wet.

The headhouse was fitted with windows that provided light when work needed to be done at the top of the elevator. The windows could be opened to provide ventilation for the grain stored in the second-floor bins. Some mills had a rather large headhouse that looked more like an extension of the roof.

MILL ECONOMICS

In the geographic area covered in this book, mills were about eight to ten miles apart. The resulting radius of ten miles would then approximately indicate the number of acres of cultivated farmland needed to support a feed mill. We know that some towns supported two feed mills, and possibly three, but keep in mind that mills didn't depend solely on milling services for local farmers. Some mill owners were grain dealers who bought grain from distant sources and shipped out their feed products.

This business model was documented in the Michigan Supreme Court case of a mill owner in Cedar Springs. During the 1911 season, he had about half a carload of rye on hand that he wanted to sell. He approached the owner of the Sand Lake mill about five miles up the track. The Sand Lake owner also had excess rye on hand and agreed to load it into the same car that the Cedar Springs owner had half filled. Neither owner had weighed the car, so they measured their rye in bushels. When the Sand Lake owner put his rye on the car, it may have filled the car nearly full. The carload was then sold to a grain depot in Buffalo, New York.

After it left Sand Lake, the car was weighed in a railroad yard in Grand Rapids and then weighed again when it reached Buffalo, where a discrepancy between the two weights was found. When the car was unloaded, the Buffalo dealer measured the rye in bushels and found a shortage of 248 bushels. For some reason, the Cedar Springs dealer paid for the shortage and then turned around and sued the Sand Lakes dealer, claiming the shortage was his fault.

The Cedar Springs dealer was awarded $264 in damages. Even accounting for the difference in dollar value between then and today, it seems a trifling sum, given the cost of the long legal deliberations. Later, the award was reversed, so it was all for nothing. The point is that the perception of a mill owner laboring in dust-covered overalls from dawn to dusk is not necessarily correct. His millhands did that as he dickered with other dealers.

Today, mill operators still have an informal network and deal among themselves to smooth out the bumps in daily operations. A simple example is a mill that has a large order to fill and a shortage of one ingredient. Calls are made until the ingredient is located and the purchase price agreed on. A similar situation may occur when a regular supplier shows up with a load of grain for which the mill has no room in their storage bins. The mill owner calls around for a buyer to take it off his hands.

Mills regularly came and went. Fire was a common destroyer. Grain dust is highly flammable, and boiler explosions in steam-operated mills were common, too. Fire insurance premiums were so high that owners could not afford it or didn't buy complete coverage. If a mill burned, that was the end of it. Mills changed owners regularly, too, and some went bankrupt. In recent years, many mills have been converted to farm and garden supply stores. A recent count of operating feed mills in Minnesota totaled more than 1,000. We can infer that there were probably at least that many in Michigan.

Population growth and suburban sprawl has taken a toll on local feed mills. Highways now allow a farmer to ship his grain wherever he can receive the highest price. So, if a feed mill becomes unprofitable or closes for another reason, it is unlikely that it will be sold or that a new mill will start up. Unless the buy local movement makes increasing inroads into the agricultural system, there is nothing on the horizon to stem the loss of small mills.

HOW TO FIND FEED MILLS

• Drive through the rural areas surrounding your community. The country roads are pleasant and uncrowded, though you may have to follow a slow-moving tractor towing a farm implement for a while. Look around in the small towns you pass through. If there is a railroad, drive along it and you may happen upon a grain mill. It is likely that a town will even have a Railroad Street. Even if you don't turn up a feed mill you will probably see an interesting old church, notable mansion, or pretty park.

• Check with local historical societies. There are far more of these than you might expect. They network with each other and can direct you to a historical society in a different area. If you find a feed mill and are curious about it, the historical society probably has a file containing old photos of the mill. Most historical societies have limited hours, so call before you make the drive.

• When you find a working mill, ask about other mills in the vicinity. The feed mill operators know each other and will not only direct you to another mill, but may have information about it.

• Do a Google search of feed mills in your state or county. You may have to wade through a lot of sites that are advertisements for farm stores, and be wary of anything called Old Mill Restaurant, as it may simply be located on the site of a mill that once existed. In that case, the best you can hope for is a photo of the old mill on the wall.

• Join a SPOOM chapter. The Society for the Preservation of Old Mills has regional and local chapters scattered around the country. They sponsor regular field trips, some quite lengthy, to both private and preserved mills, and sometimes offer support to people studying old mills.

FEED MILLS ARE ARTIFACTS OF THE PAST.
The ornate train stations are gone; the automobile did them in.
The great steamships are gone; the airplane is responsible for that.
One thing is sure—people and their farm animals will always need to eat.
So there will always be farms that grow grain and an industry to process it.

WHY NOT GO OUT AND ENJOY THE OLD FEED MILLS WHILE YOU STILL CAN?

EPILOGUE

When I began photographing mills decades ago, it was not obvious that the mills were nearing the end of their lives. Time passed, and now and then a mill would close, but that had always been the case. Their disappearance was slow at first, but then became more obvious. My early interest in mills was largely in their visual appearance. They made engaging subjects for photographs. However, I couldn't help occasionally meeting the owners or workers on the scene, and I learned more about the feed mill business from each of the encounters. Over time, our conversations were more in-depth. What came across was a general air of resignation, born of the reality of changes in the agricultural economy.

One mill operator told me about his brother who had operated a nursery and garden supply store. "When they opened the Walmart down the road and it had a garden center, it was over for my brother," he said. The farm-and-home chains have usurped much of the feed mill sale of farm supplies. Farmers now sell their produce on contract to large corporations who pick it up from the farmers' storage bins. They don't take it to the local feed mill anymore.

Some mills have adapted by growing their own business in a way that allows them to work in much the same way as the corporations. They may make it work. The eat local movement is pressuring grocery chains to offer locally produced food. Grocery chains, though, are faced with daunting competitive pressures of their own. They cannot supply all their stores with produce from scattered small farms.

I wish it could be otherwise. We live in a time of expanding population, both at home and around the world. Science and technology advances have been able to keep up with milling needs so far, but it isn't clear what part small milling operations will play in these advances.

Now, when I visit a small or medium-sized mill, it is often to photograph an abandoned site, to record it before it is demolished. It was a good ride while it lasted.

ACKNOWLEDGMENTS

So many people, in the mills and the towns around them, spoke kindly and patiently with me, and I cannot remember them all. There were times when the exchange was brief, only a few words, but the information turned out to be golden. To all these folks, I extend apologies. The following people spent generous amounts of time helping me complete this book and allowed me to photograph their facilities and interview their employees for publication.

Ron Camp, Edmore, Michigan, cared enough to preserve the memory and images of his mill.

Sam Gebhardt, owner for twenty years of Cedar Springs Mill and Supply, has demonstrated in an enviable manner how dedication to a purpose and his customers' needs can maintain an important tradition.

Harley Sietsema, Allendale, Michigan, for graciously giving me "the run of the mill" and granting kind hospitality.

Rick Rose, manager of Sietsema Farms mill, Howard City, was welcoming and helpful. I count him a friend to me and the industry he serves.

Randy Spees, manager of County Line Farms in Trufant, Michigan, shared his extensive knowledge of the feed mill craft and directed me to important discoveries.

Cesar Hernandez, whose high energy was very much in evidence at the Walcott Elevator and who cleared up many mysteries about feed mill operations for me.

Dwayne Ruthig, CEO and general manager, Caledonia Farmers Elevator, who corrected several mistakes and filled in many gaps in my knowledge of mill operations.

Tom Haradine, retired owner of Harvey's Mill in Carson City. Tom's nearly encyclopedic knowledge of mill operations and fascinating anecdotes fueled my interest and concentration on the subjects of this book.

Dan Leach, manager, Mid-Michigan Specialty Crops LLC, in Ithaca, who made sure I had covered all the most interesting points in his facility.

Finally, thanks to the crews at the mills, the folks at the historical societies, and everyone who encouraged me in this endeavor.